MW00593505

IN YOUR EYES

IN YOUR EYES

Quotations on Gay Love

EDITED BY

Richard M. Derus

A STONEWALL INN BOOK
ST. MARTIN'S PRESS NEW YORK

ACKNOWLEDGMENTS

No book is ever possible without the kind support and firm guidance of a respected editor.
Mine was Keith Kahla, a friend of many years'
standing. It's a testament to the tolerance of
Claudia Menza, friend and business partner, that
I lived to finish this collection of quotes. She
endured many missed meetings with much more
good grace than my wildest fantasies could con-
jure. Thanks also to Robert Cloud, whose help
and suggestions have proved invaluable.

Wonderful friends, too numerous to present
by name, have taught me the all-too-uncommon
lesson that romance isn't confined to lovers. In
fact, romance is most valuable, most wonderful,
when it comes in unexpectedly, wearing a familiar suit, and makes *just* the right remark—every-
day magic, more valuable for precisely that.

The quotes I've included in this book show the commonality of love's expressions. Literature contains so many beautiful passages on love and romance in all its forms, it was difficult for me to choose only a few. These are, of necessity, the highly idiosyncratic selections of one gay man. Of course, I hope they will speak to everyone, of every persuasion.

—RICHARD M. DERUS

IN YOUR EYES

The memory of you
will always remain.

A tear—
a perfect crystal
shattered.

—CHRISTOPHER MAYNARD

FIRST LOVE

April's First-Born Flowers

SONNET 21

So is it not with me as with that Muse
Stirr'd by a painted beauty to his verse,
Who heaven itself for ornament doth use
And every fair with his fair doth rehearse,
Making a couplement of proud compare,
With sun and moon, with earth and sea's rich
    gems,
With April's first-born flowers, and all things
    rare
That heaven's air in this huge rondure hems.
O let me, true in love, but truly write,
And then believe me, my love is as fair
As any mother's child, though not so bright
As those gold candles fix'd in heaven's air:
    Let them say more that like of hear-say well;
    I will not praise that purpose not to sell.

—WILLIAM SHAKESPEARE

Holding him was like holding some improbable gardenia, something at once noble and sensual—which must be the definition of "romantic." I'd thought about him so long that he'd become nearly mythic for me, so that it was his actual presence that was the improbability, like the host which is at one and the same time Our Lord's body and a nearly tasteless wafer. . . . The insertion of a myth into a precise moment and place is both miraculous and fairly humorous.

—EDMUND WHITE, from "Watermarked"

They are wrong who say that love is blind. On the contrary, nothing—not even the smallest detail—escapes the eyes; one sees everything in the loved one, notices everything; but melts it all into one flame with the great and simple: "I love you."

—HENRYK SIENKIEWICZ

Bob laughed and suddenly grabbed him. They clung to one another. Jim was overwhelmingly conscious of Bob's body. For a moment they pretended to wrestle. Then both stopped. Yet each continued to cling to the other as though waiting for a signal to break or to begin again. For a long time neither moved. Smooth chests touching, sweat mingling, breathing fast in unison.

Abruptly, Bob pulled away. For a bold moment their eyes met. Then, deliberately, gravely, Bob shut his eyes and Jim touched him, as he had so many times in dreams, without words, without thought, without fear. When the eyes are shut, the true world begins.

As faces touched, Bob gave a shuddering sigh and gripped Jim tightly in his arms. Now they were complete, each became the other, as their bodies collided with a primal violence, like to like, metal to magnet, half to half and the whole restored.

—GORE VIDAL, from *The City and the Pillar*

Give me a boy whose face and hand
Are rough with dust and circus-sand
Whose ruddy flesh exhales the scent
Of health without embellishment;
Sweet to my sense is such a youth,
Whose charms have all the charm of truth.

—STRATO

All they that love not tobacco and boys are
fools.

—CHRISTOPHER MARLOWE

The divine magnet is on you, and my magnet
responds. Which is the biggest? A foolish question—they are *One*.

—HERMAN MELVILLE, to Nathaniel Hawthorne

I was alone of the top deck of Vic's bus for the first time. I sat in the back seat, impatient for his arrival, excited and apprehensive.

"What you reading?" he asked, sitting down beside me and putting his arm round my shoulders.

"You don't mind me doing this, do you?"

My heartfelt "No" came out in a whisper.

"You're all nerves, Pete."

"Yes," I agreed.

"You're shaking. Calm down."

He kissed me, then, very quickly, on my right ear, which tingled from the shock.

The bus stopped, and Vic withdrew his arm. "Work to do," he said, and left me alone on the now-magical back seat.

—PAUL BAILEY, from *An Immaculate Mistake*

If it be a sin to love a lovely lad,
Oh then sin I.

—RICHARD BARNFIELD

The magic of first love is the ignorance that
it can ever end.

—TUSCAN PROVERB

When first I met you
in all your sudden beauty,
your eyes sparkled like
diamonds
on a jeweler's black velvet.
Elongated corners
of delicate ellipses
hinting at noble lineage
sprung from antiquity.

Windows
shining in dark night
marking an abode
drew me near.
With joyous laughter
the house overflowed.

Filled libraries
which might have put
Alexandria to shame—
burning, anticipating
your fair smile.

Quickly you
go into thick
velvet night
the waiting world
barring from me your
most exquisite beauty.

—CHRISTOPHER MAYNARD

Suspicious of my simplest acts I grow;
 I doubt my passing words, however brief;
 I catch his glances feeling like a thief.
Perchance he wonders why I shun him so,—
It would be strange indeed if he should know
 I love him, love him, love him past belief!

—JOHN GAMBRIL NICHOLSON

In the charming season of the flower-time of
    youth,
Thou shalt love boys, yearning for their thighs
    and honeyed mouth.

      —SOLON

Nothing, nothing else in the world, can warm
my soul now except to write poems of you.

      —VILHELM EKELUND

A double brightness burned me: rays
There were which travelled in the gaze
Of that boy's eyes, the beams of Love;
And others from the Sun above.

      —MELEAGER

Dargelos' presence drove me out of my mind. I avoided him. I lay in wait for him. I dreamt of some miracle which would bring his attention to bear on me, disencumber him of his vainglory, reveal to him the real meaning of my attitude, which, as things stood, he had necessarily to view as some sort of preposterous prudishness and which was nothing short of an insane desire to please him.

—JEAN COCTEAU

Cold in my professions, warm in my friendships, I wish, my Dear Laurens, it might be in my power, by action rather [than] words, to convince you that I love you. I shall only tell you that 'till you bade us Adieu, I hardly knew the value you had taught my heart to set upon you.

—ALEXANDER HAMILTON, letter to John Laurens

Love is a haughty despot; he will have all or
nothing.

— STENDHAL

True love is like a sigh from the heart; it teaches
in a moment everything one ought to say.

— CORNEILLE

Gossip grows like weeds
In a summer meadow.
My love and I
Sleep arm in arm.

— CLASSIC JAPANESE LOVE POEM

We wrestled, kissed, and held each other so close he seemed to be a part of me, working in symmetry. His broad shoulders surrounded me with protective warmth. Tender passion flushed through me, filling long-forgotten places. Sharing every softness, exposing every weakness, we trusted each other's arms.

—JAMES D. WAGONER, from "The White Knight Is Dead"

He who has been smitten by the arrows of love never again fears any other wound.

—GUARINI

The heart needs its surfeit of abundance. Enough can never be enough again.

—KONRAD FERDINAND MEYER

Like all forms of love, homosexuality remains mysterious and eludes our total understanding. Like all forms of love, it is a longing for a lost attachment.

—RICHARD ISAY, from *Being Homosexual*

Sweet boy, gentle boy,
Don't be ashamed, you are mine forever:
The same rebellious fire is in both of us,
We are living one life.

I am not afraid of mockery:
Between us, the two have become one,
We are precisely like a double nut
Under a single shell.

—GABRIEL GILLET

The heart has reasons that the mind knows not.

—PASCAL

My attraction and affection for Peter was immediate, was absolutely primitive, explosive, visceral, impassioned, and dreamlike, all at the same time. . . .

—Stanley Siegel, from *Uncharted Lives*

He was scared of how sexy he found Lyle, afraid of alienating Lyle with his desire. He found almost everything about Lyle sexy; his body, his mind, his talk, the way he climbed the stairs, the way his fingers gripped a fork, blushing with tension, the way he smelled and tasted, the impossibly soft way his back and neck and shoulders congregated, the spot there, the crux of him, naked and lickable.

—Peter Cameron, from *The Weekend*

Love is blinding. That is why lovers like to touch.

—German proverb

He was too busy marvelling at the Brother's face and the colour of it. Before he had thought it was the deepest black, but in this, he now realised, he had been mistaken. His skin was dark brown. It had a matt patina upon it which made it seem like some sheer velvet. His ears were very small and hugged his head. . . . If he had a choice, he thought, those were the ears he would choose. The Brother's hair, which he had thought was just a dense cap of black, was in fact, from this perspective, a soft halo. He wondered if he touched it how it would feel. Then, when [the Brother] turned, he saw his face in profile. The nose, quite flat and wide when viewed full-face, in profile was sculpted and honed, a perfect concave arc from the bridge to the tip. At that angle he looked much younger—almost like a child. And from [the Brother's] full mouth came the sound which mesmerized him and made him shiver. So deeply affected was he by the tone of the voice that he could not concentrate on the meaning of his words.

—MICHAEL CARSON, from *Brothers in Arms*

You long to stir in me desire,
And urge me to the joys of love?
Loose all the words of passion's fire
Upon me, if my heart you'd move!

—HORACE

I arise from dreams of thee
In the first sweet sleep of night,
When the winds are breathing low,
And the stars are shining bright.

—PERCY BYSSHE SHELLEY

I am on fire with that soft sound
  You make, in uttering my name.

—JAMES ELROY FLECKER

The less my hope, the greater my love.

—TERENCE

He who often says "I love not" is in love.

—OVID

"He could wipe the floor with me,
Or kick me, he couldn't kill my love,
Even if he'd broken my back
He'd only have to ask a kiss
And my troubles would disappear. . . ."

—FRANÇOIS VILLON

Love is selfishness for two.

—DE LA SALLE

center in paler gray, ice green, turquoise, sienna, amethyst, even lemon yellow. From the tiny perfect knob under his knee that connected the two long muscles running beneath his thigh down into the one that ran below his calf, to the nearly feathered tiny V's of hair that made up his sideburns, I'd never before encountered such an idealization of form, or, more impressively, such a lavish extravagance of detail! As though once he'd been shaped, his Creator had been so surprised, so pleased with the result, He'd come back again and again, dotingly, to touch up his Work.

—FELICE PICANO, from *Like People in History*

What he did ardently, painfully want was that just as he was, Hans Hansen should love him; and he wooed Hans Hansen in his own way, deeply, lingeringly, devotedly, with a melancholy that gnawed and burned more terribly than all the sudden passion one might have expected from his exotic looks.

—THOMAS MANN, from *Tonio Kröger*

The Page of Herodias: He was my brother, and nearer to me than a brother. I gave him a little box full of perfumes, and a ring of agate that he wore always on his hand. In the evening we were wont to walk by the river, and among the almond trees, and he used to tell me of the things of his country. He spake ever very low. The sound of his voice was like the sound of the flute, of one who playeth upon the flute.

—Oscar Wilde, from *Salomé*

It was strange to see someone you have only known alone begin interacting with other people, for that somebody to you disappears and is replaced by a different, more complex person. You watch him revolve in this new company, revealing new facets, and there is nothing you can do but hope you like these other sides as much as you like the side that seemed whole when it faced only you.

—Peter Cameron, from *The Weekend*

There is no love so true as one which dies
  untold.

I search the land and seas
For a man that I may love.
Whenever my heart finds him,
Then he'll have found his slave.

And seek forever more the soul's impossible
  bliss.

SONNET 46

Mine eye and heart are at a mortal war,
How to divide the conquest of thy sight;
Mine eye my heart thy picture's sight would
bar,
My heart mine eye the freedom of that right.
My heart doth plead that thou in him dost
lie,—
A closet never pierc'd with crystal eyes,—
But the defendant doth that plea deny,
And says in him thy fair appearance lies.
To 'cide this title is impanelled
A quest of thoughts, all tenants to the heart;
And by their verdict is determined
The clear eye's moiety and the dear heart's
part,
  As thus—mine eye's due is thine outward
  part,
  And my heart's right thine inward love of
  heart.

—WILLIAM SHAKESPEARE

Oh, my love life would be so happy if it were only spectatorship, but it is in fact only envy.

—GLENWAY WESTCOTT, from *Continual Lessons*

Love is the most selfish of all emotions, and so the least generous when hurt.

—BENJAMIN CONSTANT

The lover who sets out on the road of love with no money is in for more labors than Hercules.

—PLAUTUS

One who loves with passion cannot easily forgive.

—PAUL CLAUDEL

A lover always believes that which he fears.

—OVID

Though I have been in love a good many times, I have never experienced the bliss of requited love. I have most loved people who cared little or nothing for me.

—W. SOMERSET MAUGHAM

Jealousy is the shadow of love. The greater the love, the longer the shadow.

—POLISH PROVERB

It is hard to suddenly stop loving someone. It is hard, but somehow you will succeed.

—CATULLUS

SONNET 39

O, how thy worth with manners may I sing,
When thou art all the better part of me?
What can mine own praise to mine own self
    bring?
And what is 't but mine own when I praise
    thee?
Even for this let us divided live,
And our dear love lose name of single one,
That by this separation I may give
That due to thee, which thou deserv'st alone.
O absence! what a torment wouldst thou prove,
Were it not thy sour leisure gave sweet leave
To entertain the time with thoughts of love,
Which time and thoughts so sweetly doth
    deceive,
    And that thou teachest how to make one
      twain,
    By praising him here who doth hence
      remain.

—WILLIAM SHAKESPEARE

The technique of a great seducer requires a facility and an indifference in passing from one object of affection to another. . . . The desire to count up exactly the riches which each new love brings us, and to see it change, and perhaps to watch it grow old, accords ill with a multiplicity of conquests.

—MARGUERITE YOURCENAR, from *The Memoirs of Hadrian*

Whenever I behold someone who possesses any talent or displays any dexterity of mind, who can do or say something more appropriately than the rest of the world, I am compelled to fall in love with him; and then I give myself up to him so entirely that I am no longer my own property, but wholly his.

—MICHELANGELO

If a man urge me to tell wherefore I loved him,
I feel it cannot be expressed, but by answering:
Because it was he, because it was my self.

—MICHEL DE MONTAIGNE

Night and day you are the one. . . .

—COLE PORTER, from *Gay Divorce*

Malcolm, I love thee more than women love
And pure and warm and equal is the feeling
which binds us and our destinies forever.

—RALPH WALDO EMERSON, from *Journals*,
Vol. 1

Nothing, I suppose, is as powerful for me as the idea of actually living with someone; "living" and "sleeping" are transitive verbs for me, intimate and cherishing ones.

—EDMUND WHITE, from "Watermarked"

There comes one moment, once—and God
      help those
Who pass that moment by!—when Beauty
      stands
Looking into the soul with grave, sweet eyes
That sicken at pretty words!

—EDMOND ROSTAND, from *Cyrano de Bergerac*

Love may be delayed but not destroyed.

—PROPERTIUS

Love is the currency minted in God's bank.

—GIACCONE

The power of love is determined by the
strength the heart has given it.

—ITALIAN PROVERB

At long last love has come, love such that to
conceal it would shame it more than proclaim
it.

—SULPICIA

Despite the difficulties of my story, despite dis-
comforts, doubts, despairs, despite impulses to
be done with it, I unceasingly affirm love. . . .

—ROLAND BARTHES, from *A Lover's Discourse*

"Imagine that out of all these years in New York, the person who finally gives me the love I'm supposedly searching for is a crazy kid who worked at the airport in Newark and doesn't read because it makes him fall asleep. And who can fall asleep in discotheques! As he used to do. And who only wants one thing in life—a lover. Someone he can buy presents for and be utterly faithful to. Nothing in life is ever where you look for it!"

—ANDREW HOLLERAN, from *Nights in Aruba*

The sound of a kiss is not as loud as that of a cannon but its echo may endure much longer.

—ITALIAN PROVERB

Love hath no measurement in time; it buds and blooms and ripens in one glowing hour.

—THEODOR KOERNER

Nothing except true and equal love takes the
  curse off of desire.

—GLENWAY WESTCOTT, from *Continual Lessons*

I thee, both as man and woman, prize;
For a perfect love implies
Love in all capacities

—ABRAHAM COWLEY

"Love seeketh not itself to please,
"Nor for itself hath any care
"But for another gives its ease
"And builds a heaven in hell's despair."

—WILLIAM BLAKE

———

The human soul, like the bee, extracts sweetness
even from bitter herbs.

—POLISH PROVERB

———

I turned him round in my hands, kissed the back
of his neck, stood away from him a moment as
I undid my cuffs, glancing down at his legs,
where the summer tanlines still palely showed.
I thought, I mustn't say I love you, though they
were the only words I had in my head.

—ALAN HOLLINGHURST, from *The Folding Star*

———

Life is a long sleep, and love is its dream.

—ALFRED DE MUSSET

Self-mastery must be preceded by a letting-go
of the desire to master the world. . . . Achilles,
yielding to the gods and letting go of [Patroclus],
the one dearest to him, comes in the renunciation
to repossess both his friend and himself. . . .

—THOMAS VAN NORTWICK

[He] needed love. That it was homosexual love
was, in my opinion, of no importance. It was the
only variety available and the need was crucial.
So we became lovers.

—JAMES BLAKE

Love often enters in the name of friendship.

—OVID

"Love and sex are just two steps in the same process. If I love you, I want to give you my trust, my tuna sandwich, my body. You will value my friendship and respond."

—ANONYMOUS, from *The Gay Report* by Karla Jay and Allen Young

Now love is a lean and long-legged body, its limbs still those of a teenager, soft and sinuous, and princely. Love is a long face with a strong, square jaw. Love is two bright, dark eyes, with a lock of dark honey-colored hair falling across them every so often. Love is a special way of moving the hands or letting them hang down by the legs. Last but not least, love is a voice, the pitch of a stifled kiss, the feeling of a bright, open burst of laughter. Love is the simplicity of a person's ways, the essence and gracefulness of a being who, as this dream currently stands, answers to the name of Thomas.

—PIER VITTORIO TONDELLI, from *Separate Rooms*

Love and fear exclude each other.

Turning back the covers, I found myself laughing out loud. Candy and flowers: a hideous valentine box and ghastly plastic roses, their awful taste-lessness the result of far more thought and consideration than mere hothouse flowers and designer chocolates. And I found myself oddly, unexpectedly touched. Candy and flowers indeed!

But isn't it true that love makes the world go square.

—EDWARD O. PHILLIPS, from *Sunday's Child*

Lovers always remember everything.

—OVID

"You know, I think of romance as a little gift, a little cloud that falls on two people sometimes. It's just a certain clicking. And maybe that has to do with the passion from years ago . . . maybe it's a refinement of that. And . . . then there's the friendship."

—"TIMMY," from *Decent Passions* by Michael Denneny

We split the check, our first time doing so in many years, maybe ten years. The waitress takes the money. She goes. We don't get up. The whole time Robert holds my hand. Our meal is just getting going. He presses his lips together. A waiter takes an order next to us, looking at us. It gets dark outside. The palm trees brace against the wind, shaking a bit on top. Robert holds my hand. We look. Sitting quietly into the meal, as it digests in us, the fears about how we would leave the restaurant, and the sense that we would leave it, but only for now. We sit quietly. The house in Venice near the ocean is emptied of dog barks, meals. The books divided up. The voices, placated. Now just us. There was a visit. Now the man who had never spoken to me of visits is sitting here, visiting. His hand on mine, in the now-empty restaurant. We sit still, hands clasped and lips silent. The words will come. Not now, but soon. Through the lips. Like a kiss. Like a breath. Like a wish. Like a riot. Like a voice from another world. Like anyone who knows anymore.

—DOUGLAS SADOWNICK, from *Sacred Lips of the Bronx*

—

We loved each other in the way we do
    And never spoke about it, Al & me,
But we both *knowed*, and knowin' it so true
    Was more than any woman's kiss could be.

—BADGER CLARK, from "The Lost Pardner"

Against my love shall be, as I am now,
With Time's injurious hand crush'd and
    o'erworn;
When hours have drain'd his blood and fill'd
    his brow
With lines and wrinkles; when his youthful
    morn
Hath travell'd on to age's steepy night;
And all those beauties whereof now he's king
Are vanishing or vanish'd out of sight
Stealing away the treasure of his spring;
For such a time do I now fortify
Against confounding age's cruel knife,
That he shall never cut from memory
My sweet love's beauty, though my lover's life:
  His beauty shall in these black lines be seen,
  And they shall live, and he in them still
    green.

—WILLIAM SHAKESPEARE

COUPLEHOOD

Still Constant in a Wondrous

Excellence

SONNET 105

Let not my love be call'd idolatry,
Nor my beloved as an idol show,
Since all alike my songs and praises be
To one, of one, still such, and ever so.
Kind is my love to-day, to-morrow kind,
Still constant in a wondrous excellence;
Therefore my verse, to constancy confin'd,
One thing expressing, leaves out difference.
"Fair, kind, and true," is all my argument,
"Fair, kind, and true," varying to other words;
And in this change is my invention spent,
Three themes in one, which wondrous scope
    affords.
   "Fair, kind, and true" have often liv'd alone,
    Which three till now never kept seat in one.

—WILLIAM SHAKESPEARE

"Tomorrow with dawn I must attend
In yonder vale." "What for?" "Why ask? A
    friend
Takes him a husband there and bids a few
Be present." Wait awhile and we shall view
Such contracts formed without shame or fear
And entered on the records of the year.

—JUVENAL

Grow old along with me!
The best is yet to be,
The last of life, for which the first was made.

—ROBERT BROWNING

Love is blind, but marriage restores one's
    vision.

—ITALIAN PROVERB

Love is . . . born with the pleasure of looking at each other, it is fed with the necessity of seeing each other, it is concluded with the impossibility of separation!

—José Martí

If you have a hankering to be formally bonded, don't be ashamed. Go for it! Chart out a game plan, find that man of your dreams and claim him.

—Craig G. Harris

Love one another, but make not a bond of
    love:
Let it rather be a moving sea between the
    shores of your souls.

—Kahlil Gibran, from *The Prophet*

There are many evils in love: suspicions, quarrels, wrongs, and injustices, but war precedes peace.

—TERENCE

Love makes difficult things easy and almost unworthy of note.

—LATIN PROVERB

Visible gay couples are rare role models and should strive to present the best possible impression.

—BRYAN MONTE

No rival can take my love away; it is sure and today's splendor will last forever.

—PROPERTIUS

It is often said how necessary for the ordinary marriage is some public recognition of the relation, and some accepted standard of conduct in it. May not, to a lesser degree, something of the same kind be true of the homogenic attachment? It has had its place as a recognized and guarded institution in the elder and more primitive societies; and it seems quite probable that a similar place will be accorded it in the societies of the future.

—EDWARD CARPENTER

He seemed to take to me quite as naturally and unbiddenly as I to him; and when our smoke was over, he pressed his forehead against mine, clasped me round the waist, and said that henceforth we were married; meaning, in his country's phrase, that we were bosom friends; he would gladly die for me, if need should be.

—HERMAN MELVILLE, from *Moby-Dick*

Happy are those held by an unbroken bond of love that will not be separated before death.

—HORACE

Same-sex relationships are no more problematic but no easier than any other human relationships. They are in many ways the same and in several ways different from heterosexual relationships but in themselves are no less possible or worthwhile.

—CHRISTOPHER LARKIN

The primary difference between a heterosexual marriage and a homosexual relationship is that the law covers the operation of one and has nothing to do with the other.

—MARK SENAK

It's easier facing the world as two people rather than one.

—Robert Ferro

Alan: When I said that I loved you before, you didn't answer me.
Arnold: I didn't realize it was a question.

—Harvey Fierstein, from *Torch Song Trilogy*

One of the frequent myths created by both the heterosexual and gay worlds is that gay lovers don't remain together. It is shocking how many young gay men believe this to be true.

—Charles Silverstein

Come and let us live, my dear. . . . Let us love
and fear not what the old men might say.

—CATULLUS

If there were only some way of contriving that
a state or an army should be made up of lovers
and their loves, they would be the very best
governors of their own city, abstaining from all
dishonor, and emulating one another in honor;
and when fighting at each other's side, although
a mere handful, they would overcome the world.

—PLATO, from *The Symposium*

Love me a little as long as you love me long.

—ITALIAN PROVERB

We all knew that these rituals were the result of a long process of accommodation by which two men of strong wills and complex temperaments had worked out a way to live together, had made themselves a home. As in other couples, there had been jealousies, infidelities, and moments when each other wondered whether it was worth going on, but they had found solutions and made affirmations. We felt this history when we assembled for tea, and we understood that every object in that apartment had its own intimate story related to its discovery, its purchase, and the place that had been chosen for it next to all the other objects of a shared life. We joked about [them] being such creatures of habit, yet the feeling they conveyed to their guests and friends was one of peace, hard won perhaps and based on innumerable compromises but also built firmly on respect and a very deep love.

—GEORGE STAMBOLIAN on writers ROBERT FERRO and MICHAEL GRUMLEY

New loves come and go, an old love remains.

—Tuscan proverb

In the summer of 1984 Roger and I were in Greece together, and for both of us it was a peak experience that left us dazed and slightly giddy. We'd been together for ten years, and life was very sweet. On the high bluff of ancient Thera, looking out across the southern Aegean toward Africa, my hand grazed a white marble block covered edge to edge with Greek characters, line after precise line. The marble was tilted face up to the weather, its message slowly eroding in the rain. "I hope somebody's recorded all this," I said, realizing with a dull thrill of helplessness that this was the record, right here on this stone.

When I began to write about AIDS during Roger's illness, I wanted a form that would move with breathless speed, so I could scream if I wanted and rattle on and empty my Uzi into the air. The marbles of Greece kept coming back to my mind. By the time Roger died the form was set—not quite marble, not quite Greek—but it was in my head that if only a fragment remained in the future, to fade in the sulphurous rain, it would say how much I loved him and how terrible was the calamity.

—PAUL MONETTE, from the introduction to
Borrowed Time

He was losing his best friend, the witness to his life. The skill for enjoying a familiar pleasure about to disappear was hard to acquire. It was sort of like sex. If you were just unconsciously rocking in the groove you missed the kick, but if you kept mentally shouting "Wow!" you shot too soon. Knowing how to appreciate the rhythms of these last casual moments—to cherish them while letting them stay casual—demanded a new way of navigating time.

—EDMUND WHITE, from "Palace Days"

Love is such a great happiness that even the darkest is still interspersed with beams of light.

—POLISH PROVERB

Edward: He's gone, and for his absence thus
    I mourn.
Did never sorrow go so near my heart,
As doth the want of my sweet Gaveston.
And could my crown's revenue bring him
    back,
I would freely give it to his enemies,
And think I gained, having bought so dear a
    friend.

—CHRISTOPHER MARLOWE, from *Edward II*

True love despises and will not tolerate decay.

—SENECA

We, Peter Didaz and Munio Vandilaz, make a pact and agreement mutually between ourselves for the house and church of St. Mary of Ordines, which we jointly own and in which we share the labor, taking care of visitors and in regulating the care of, decorating and governing the premises, planting and building. And we share equally in the work of the garden, and in feeding and clothing ourselves and supporting ourselves. And we agree that neither of us may give to anyone else without the other's consent anything, on account of our friendship, and that we will divide the work on the house evenly, and assign labor equally and support our workers equally and with dignity. And we will remain good friends to each other with faith and sincerity, and with other people [we will remain equally] friends and enemies all days and nights, forever. And if Peter dies before Munio he will leave Munio the property and the documents. And if Munio dies before Peter he will leave him the house and the documents.

—DOCUMENT OF A.D. 1031, from the Cartulary of Celanova

Love is the longing to achieve another's happiness
by achieving our own.

—ITALIAN PROVERB

I have a husband, and we have a dog, and we
live in the country. It's what I've always wanted.

—TERRY SWEENY

The happiness of being in love sweetens whatever
pain exists.

—FOSCOLO

When lovers get angry, their love revives.

—TERENCE

Love is a smoke rais'd with the fume of sighs;
Being purg'd, a fire sparkling in lovers' eyes.

—WILLIAM SHAKESPEARE